Creating Wellness at Home and in School

by
William A. Howatt

ISBN 0-87367-689-0
Copyright © 2001 by the Phi Delta Kappa Educational Foundation
Bloomington, Indiana

This fastback is sponsored by the
Ball State University Chapter
of Phi Delta Kappa International,
which made a generous contribution
toward publication costs.

Table of Contents

Introduction

Remember Gumby? He was the little green guy from the children's cartoon who could bend and stretch in unimaginable ways. Today's teachers are expected to be like Gumby — to bend many different ways simultaneously. But as professionals, they also are expected to be in control and never to admit their limitations. Even when teachers are working to maximum levels, they are asked to do more without compromising quality.

In a study published in the *International Journal of Stress Management*, 67% of teachers surveyed describe their jobs as "extremely stressful." Because teaching is a helping profession, teachers are intensely involved with their students and often do not take the best care of themselves (Maslach 1982). New requirements, such as tests, and new technologies have added even more pressures to teachers' jobs.

However, regardless of new pressures and changes in the education environment, one thing remains the same: Teachers who perceive themselves as balanced will be more effective in the classroom.

This fastback addresses the issue of stress by providing teachers with a resource guide that 1) defines stress, 2) normalizes the origins of teacher stress, 3) provides a model for achieving personal wellness through life balance, and 4) provides tools for reducing the effects of stress.

Learning healthy habits can help teachers cope with the demands of their profession (Meichenbaum 1985). Teachers who take good care of themselves are better able to facilitate learning. The ultimate goal of this fastback, therefore, is to help teachers meet the challenges of teaching by demonstrating how to deal with stress effectively.

What Is Stress?

Stress is a modern term, though the phenomenon is nothing new in the teaching profession. As early as 1933 Hicks noted that 17% of a sample of 600 teachers reported they usually were nervous. In 1936 Peck found that 37% of the teachers he studied had nervous symptoms.

We now talk about stress more openly and in somewhat different terms. But talking is rarely enough to address the problems created by stress. In fact, talking about it but not doing something about it may even increase stress. When we focus on something, we can expand it. If your focus is stress, you will discover more stress and have more stress in your life. A more productive way to address stress is to know what it is and how to reduce its effects.

We can offset stress more easily if we address it before it becomes deeply rooted in our minds and bodies. Dealing with stress is like dieting. It is easier to lose 10 pounds than to lose 40. The time to address stress is *before* it becomes a major life issue, before you suffer a physical or emotional breakdown. The good news is it is never too late to *start* moving toward a more enriching life. According to Clement (1999), teachers can minimize the detrimental effects of stress in their lives by identifying the causes of stress and learning how to apply stress management techniques.

Brewer (1991) reported that about 75% of all medical complaints are stress related, with 50% of the population suffering from at least one stress-related issue on a regular basis. But what is "stress"?

Although there is no single universally accepted definition of stress, Canadian researcher Hans Selye (1974) stated a useful one: "Stress is 'perception.' It is the demands that are imposed upon us because there are too many alternatives." He went on to say, "Stress is caused by being conscientious and hardworking." Skinner (1976) said that "stress is a cerebral reaction of a particular individual to a stimulus event."

The main effect of stress on the body can be summed up by the Stress-Adaptation Theory, which states that "stress depletes the reserve capacity of individuals, thereby increasing their vulnerability to health problems" (*Mosby's Medical, Nursing, & Allied Health Dictionary* 1998, p. 8529).

The first step in dealing with stress effectively is to become aware of our stresses and to define them for ourselves. We need to accept that stress is normal and take action before it becomes more serious and cumulative. No one is immune to the effects of stress (Watkins 1983). The truth is that in North America many of us — too many — ignore what we know about the physical and mental cost of overeating, underexercising, drinking, drugging, getting angry, and so on. We often either deny that we can experience a breakdown of the mind and body or fail to muster the internal strength to adopt a healthy lifestyle.

We all have stress. In fact, we need some stress just to get out of bed in the morning. The stress we need to be functional human beings is called *eustress* (good stress). However, most of us tune in only to *distress* — bad stress.

It may be difficult to find the perfect definition of stress, but the following acrostic helps me define the effects of stress in my own life. It is amazing how powerful this simple six-letter word can be:

S = stuck in a thought
T = tolerance for situation gone
R = real to me
E = ending to something or threatening a want
S = sick feeling in body
S = self-esteem damaged

Nathan (1994) observed that people in helping professions, such as teaching, must take care of themselves because they are exposed to risks that can become chronic problems. We need not only to talk about stress but to recognize that it is real and to take action so that we can live a healthy life and not allow stress to rule us.

Identifying Stress in Daily Life

Everyone has a different threshold for stress. What stresses you may not stress someone else. The point at which you begin to feel stressed is called your "personal frustration tolerance threshold." Our health habits and how we manage our mental states largely determine the amount of stress with which we can cope. For example, if you are stressed at work and then come home to a crying baby, you may go through the roof. However, the baby's crying is not the stress; it is a trigger that releases the manifestation — in this case, anger — of accumulated stress.

On the path to personal balance, we need to know our triggers to keep stresses from accumulating and manifestations from escalating. Taking steps to avoid triggers is easier than addressing a more pervasive stress, such as frustration over the education system.

Stress often is first created by how we think. To overcome life stress, we need to be prepared to challenge our mindset. We need to practice the art of effective or positive thinking and not allow our minds to create illusions. We need to live *in* the moment with what we can control.

Triggers can set off the "fight or flight" response identified by Selye. When this response is activated, we may experience one or more of the following physical manifestations:

- An increase in blood sugar.
- A quick conversion of glycogens (stored carbohydrates and fats) into energy to sustain high energy use.
- A sharp rise in blood pressure.
- Increased respiration to increase the body's supply of oxygen.
- Increased muscle tension for quick allocation of strength.

- Pupil dilation for visual acuity.
- A release of thrombin, a blood-clotting hormone that prevents excessive bleeding from a potential wound.

Why should we think about this? The reason is simple: Our fight-or-flight response system cannot tell if we are dealing with a two-ton elephant or a six-year-old child. It releases the same amount of chemicals. When we get stressed and our bodies go into fight-or-flight mode, our bodies overproduce biochemicals. If we react in this way to stress too often or too long, these biochemicals become toxic and weaken the body.

Recognizing Stress Triggers and Symptoms

It may take time to learn how to cope with stress. A starting point is identifying your "triggers," the things that bring on stress. To start this process of self-analysis, respond to the following questions:

1. What are two or three of your primary stress triggers — for example, a late dinner, a dirty house, things not put away where you think they should be?
2. What leads you to feel overwhelmed — for example, a group of triggers or a specific trigger?
3. What do you do when you feel stressed?

Another starting point is to consider symptoms of stress that you may be feeling. These symptoms fall into two broad categories. *Psychophysical symptoms* include: tight muscles, sweating, skin problems and itching, headaches, high blood pressure, body pains, nervous tics in eyes or hands, frequent upset stomach. *Behavioral/ emotional symptoms* include: talking fast, hurrying, avoiding people, worrying excessively, experiencing bad dreams, feeling preoccupied, being easily irritated, crying for no reason, holding a grudge, feeling tired, suffering from insomnia, lacking interests, and feeling anxious.

The "Are You Stressed?" mini-assessment is another way of considering how you feel.

Are You Stressed?

Answer "yes" or "no" to these questions:

1. Are you often nervous or tense and feel unable to re-lax?
2. Do you feel as though you are under a great deal of pressure?
3. Do you often feel overwhelmed?
4. Do you have trouble sleeping?
5. Do you feel frustrated easily?

If you answered "yes" to three or more questions, you will benefit from attending to your stress and taking action to reduce stressful feelings.

Responding to Stress

Stress is real. We must take action to live a healthy life and not allow stress to rule us. If we lack the skills to reduce or to cope with stress, then we are at its mercy. Everyone can benefit from incorporating healthy, stress-reducing habits into daily living.

More often than not, stress is learned. Therefore, a first step in reducing stress is to tackle it head-on — to unlearn it. In today's fast-paced society even a slight tendency toward perfectionism can lead one to see what is *not* working, rather than to focus on what is working. If we do this, then we train ourselves to see the negative — and eventually that is all we will see. That is *learning* stress.

What I focus on will expand and become most important. If I keep seeing only negatives and telling myself that I am stressed, then I am setting the stage for stress-related problems, such as psychosomatic illness. In fact, most doctors recognize stress as the origin of many of their patients' illnesses. The more we focus on stress without acting to alleviate it, the more it becomes ingrained in daily life and the more detrimental it becomes to our physical and mental health.

Just as we can learn to be stressed, we also can learn the opposite — we can learn how to live unstressed. Most people do not become stressed overnight. It takes time. By the same token, it will take time to learn how to shed stressful thinking and to adopt more healthful practices. All stress is manageable.

I should make it clear that the goal is to develop habits of good health, not merely stress management. Why would you want to *manage* stress? Stress management is an oxymoron. What we want to do is add the knowledge and skills to achieve a balanced and healthy life. The healthier we are, the less effect stress will have on us. We all experience stress; it is what we do with it that determines our future. We have less stress when we practice healthy habits every day.

Following are keys to a healthful daily routine:

- Plan for good health; it won't just happen.
- Eat nutritious meals; choose foods consciously for good health.
- Develop a daily exercise routine.
- Practice creating mental peace; positive reflections are essential.
- Learn restful sleep habits.

Excellent health habits are a must because they help keep life events from becoming stresses. I like the definition Artistotle used for excellence because it fits this context: "Excellence is not just an act, it is a habit."

Sources of Teacher Stress

There is no single source of teacher stress, nor any specific reason why teachers today should be feeling more stressed than teachers in the past. However, a common explanation is the general pace of education in the face of technology, which is speeding up everyone's way of life. The struggle to keep abreast of new technology affects everyone in general but teachers in particular, because it also affects the lives and learning of their students.

The common thread in stressful feelings is lack of control. Teachers cannot control technology; they cannot affect the pace of societal changes that are driven by technology. Thus it is easy for teachers to feel overwhelmed or consumed by feelings of stress at not being able to "keep up." However, allowing oneself to be "consumed" by stress will not get rid of it. William Glasser (2000) teaches that we always do the best we can and that all of our behavior is intended to help us meet our personal needs. Unfortunately, in the face of stress we sometimes behave in ways that exacerbate, rather than relieve, stress.

Teachers, in particular, often feel stressed by things beyond their control. The pervasive technology challenges are compounded by three additional types of potential stressors: societal expectations, actions by authorities, and individual perceptions. I will discuss each of these areas in a moment. But first I must reiterate Glasser's notion, which is that each individual chooses how to think and feel and act. We cannot always choose the circumstances into which we are thrust. But we can choose how we respond to those circumstances. Glasser promotes the importance of taking responsibility for oneself and one's thoughts, feelings, and actions. Rather than dwelling on what we cannot control, we must focus positively on what we can control.

Societal expectations come in several forms for teachers. The topography of classrooms is changing, in part because of technological change, particularly during the past 20 years. And the pace of change has accelerated. Technology has urged on us new expectations. Recent elections, for example, have found candidates vying for prominence as "education candidates." Parents worry whether their children are learning enough or the "right things" to prepare them for the New Economy and an increasingly high-tech job market. At the same time, the standards movement, another manifestation of education change, is raising new challenges in the name of excellence and access to high-quality education for all students.

Crime statistics and values questions also worry parents and politicians, who make them into areas that teachers must worry about. Violence, including recent school killings in Colorado and California, is a pervasive concern; and so antiviolence education and character education are often thrown into the already rich mixture of curricula. Teachers are being asked to oversee students' development in every conceivable area; and the challenges are daunting and, yes, stressful.

Actions by authorities often complicate teachers' professional lives. Although teacher supervisors usually were once teachers themselves, they sometimes forget what it was like in the classroom. Moreover, it is they who are charged to steer the school's course through the often troubled waters of societal change and parent expectations. The tug of conflicting forces ripples through the school hierarchy, affecting every individual. But often it is teachers who, in the end, are called on to shoulder the burden of responsibility for student learning and behavior. They naturally feel pulled in many directions: What does the principal want? What do parents want? What, really, do students need?

Too often teachers allow such questions to prey on their minds, filling their waking hours with anxiety that spills over into wakeful nights. Time becomes a precious commodity as days fill to overflowing. And, unlike many other professionals, teachers often face the challenges in relative isolation from their peers. Classrooms can become isolation booths. The lack of a means to share problems and find solutions collegially can be a stress builder.

Individual perceptions, however, are the ultimate determinant when it comes to stress. Do teachers perceive themselves as being successful, of coping well with the challenges? Or do they see themselves as failing, as not up to the task of teaching? In the 1980s, such researchers as Schlectly and Vance (1983) demonstrated that a staggering 40% to 45% of all new teachers leave the profession within the first four years. Huling-Austin (1986) reports that in the first year a new teacher is 2.5 times more likely to leave the teaching profession and that many more will leave in the first seven years.

Wellness and personal balance are important predictors of who succeeds during the first few years of teaching in today's schools. If teachers perceives themselves as successful, then they are more likely to feel lower stress and to be able to cope with challenges. For many, self-esteem and feelings of self-worth are tied to job competence; and that means that professional development can be an important component in a comprehensive wellness program.

Brian Tracey (2000) has shown that every dollar spent on professional development at the Motorola company results in a $30 revenue increase. There is a lesson here for education. Time, money, and effort spent helping educators gain professional competence and connect with colleagues can make a difference both in enhancing professional practice and in reducing stress.

The Time Problem

Recognizing stress and knowing how to counteract or prevent it sometimes isn't enough, especially if one believes that there isn't time to take action.

Many of us know what we need to do to be healthy, but we don't think we have time to do what is needed.

I find it interesting to ask busy teachers, "What would you do if your car had a flat tire?" They say they would fix it. Why? Because it is important to them. We need to make *ourselves* as important as our cars.

I often hear the excuse, "I don't have enough time to take care of myself." Or, "If I could manage time better, I could take better care of myself." Or, "I don't have time to take care of myself because I need to take care of others." But the real problem is not just managing time better, but managing our *states of mind* better.

Of course time is at a premium for teachers, as it is for many people in today's fast-paced world. Instead of worrying about not having enough time, which is counterproductive, effective time-managers use the time they have productively. In terms of stress, this often means "managing" our states of mind. Thus the first step is to stop allowing a presumed "lack" of time to act as another stressor.

Following are states of mind into which each of us falls at some time. They are useful categories for self-assessment.

- *Peak Performance State:* Able to do things easily and effortlessly, we are "in the zone," so to speak. This is where we want to be most of the time.
- *Crisis State:* We are acting with urgency in response to a real or perceived crisis. If we stay in this state too long, we likely will feel as though we might never catch up.
- *Unbalanced State:* We are so stressed that our self-esteem is low, and we do not feel good emotional-

ly or physically. Rather than addressing the source of the stress, we adopt damaging coping behaviors, such as smoking, taking caffeine, or taking drugs to boost our self-esteem and regain a temporary sense of control.

- *Trivial State:* We are mentally tired, and so we take up trivial tasks in an attempt to organize ourselves or appear busy. In this state, we avoid real problems. Triviality becomes, in some ways, no less negative than damaging coping behaviors.
- *Numb State:* We are so mentally fatigued that we tune out the world and vegetate. Many of us do this in front of a television or by staring off into space for extended periods of time. This behavior dissociates us from the world, so that we can momentarily stop thinking about our stresses. Unlike meditation or reflection, this state is not productive and usually does not result in resolutions made or solutions found. What usually happens is that we lose time, and the stress is still there when we come out of this state. Prolonged numbness may permutate into depression.

Monitoring our mental state is one of the most positive ways to begin to deal with stress. For example, ask yourself how you feel on a typical day. Optimal performance usually means spending at least 60% to 70% of any given day in the peak performance state. Spending 10% or so of the day in crisis may not be negative, because responding well to crises keeps our problem-solving skills sharp. This can be "good stress." It also is normal to spend some time in the other states of mind, just not too much time.

The unbalanced and trivial states bear additional mention because individuals in these states turn to negative and destructive behaviors in response to stress. People use caffeine, tobacco, alcohol, excessive food, and drugs not to remove the source of stress, but in response to feeling stressed. Addictive or negative habit-forming actions are taken up to drive out feelings of low self-esteem and lack of control. In fact, they are out-of-control personal behaviors that eventually compound feelings of stress and low self-esteem.

Steps to Wellness

Three components to achieving wellness are: balance, knowledge, and direction. *Balance* refers to the balance necessary among one's important life factors, such as money (income and expenditures), career, relationships, health, self-image, and so forth. Wellness can be achieved only from a basis of balance. *Knowledge* refers to the understandings — information, skills, and attitudes — necessary to achieve wellness. *Direction* refers to assessing one's stresses and then bringing to bear the knowledge necessary to overcome them, actively responding to stressors and directing one's efforts toward achieving wellness. These three components all must be present.

Balancing life factors, acquiring knowledge about how to deal with stress and achieve wellness, and taking a positive direction are personal choices. We can benefit from Stephen Covey's (1989) concept that we can control only personal choices and actions, not the external forces that bear on our lives. In relatively few instances can we affect external forces, but we can control how we respond to those forces that we cannot affect. William Glasser, in *Choice Theory* (1998), reiterates this point: We can take charge only of what *we* do. We cannot change what others do, not by complaining and certainly not by worrying.

A major step to wellness is acquiring what I call "a habit of health." This habit is a focus on the three components I outlined: balance, knowledge, and direction. A habit of health serves both to prevent wellness problems and to repair damaged wellness. Think of wellness like a car. We put oil in the car to prevent engine problems. And when we experience car trouble, we diagnose the problem and apply a solution. Wellness is achieved in the same way as good car "health," by attending to both prevention and care.

A New Beginning

René Descartes reminded us, "I think; therefore I am." Wellness begins in reflection. We must think about our lives: How do we balance our life factors? What stresses us? How can we reduce feelings of stress? What direction must we take?

Because the three components must be viewed holistically, it may seem that we must do everything at once. To some extent, this is true. But it is important to recognize that each action, however specific, adds to that whole, which in the end is wellness. Remember, awareness and even motivation are not sufficient. To achieve wellness one must adopt a positive direction. One must take action. Following is a process for taking action.

Step 1. Choosing to Act

Begin with self-questioning. What do I want to improve in terms of health, either emotional or physical? What issues must I resolve? What circumstances should I work to change? Start with one stressor and develop a plan of action. Because stressors become habitual, focus on changing that habit and adopting a "habit of health." But remember that changing habits takes time, and be patient with yourself.

Step 2. Assessing Motivation

Reflect on why you need to take action. What compels you toward a new habit of health? What reasons or actions will help sustain you in the effort to change? The act of changing one's habits can be difficult, and the change process may be lengthy. Therefore it is important to be clear about not only the need for change but also its compelling reasons, which can help you stay focused in the positive direction.

Step 3. Making a Plan

A chain is forged one link at a time. So, too, is wellness achieved one step at a time. Write those steps down. Make them concrete. By so doing, it will be easier to sustain motivation and to ensure focus on the positive direction you have chosen. A good way to put your plan on paper is to construct a chart similar to the one illustrated.

Goals	Tasks	Dates and Times
1.		
2.		
3.		

In the *Goals* column, write down specifically what you plan to achieve. Then, in the *Tasks* column, write down those actions you will take in order to achieve each goal. Keep the goals and tasks focused and practical; they have to be doable or they won't get done. Finally, in the *Dates and Times* column, set deadlines for accomplishing the goals and tasks — and stick to them.

Step 4. Acquiring New Knowledge

Ask yourself as you plan: What do I need to learn in order to be successful in this plan? Where should I go for information? It is important to acquire new information as you need it. If money management is a stressor, how will you acquire new ideas and strategies for better managing financial matters? If fitness is a wellness goal, how should you go about gathering information that best suits your fitness needs? Where are the resources: a bank? a financial counselor? a local gym? a personal fitness trainer?

Step 5. Processing the Habit

Before a new habit of health is established, adherence to the new habit can be precarious. Acquiring a new habit is like learning to ride a bicycle. Finding one's balance and moving forward occur simultaneously. But the real trick is to keep pedaling. Therefore it pays to reflect on the sorts of challenges that might be distractors. Another question: If you do get off track, how (or what) will get you back on? Think and plan.

Step 6. Tracking Progress

The chart I recommended in Step 3 is one way to track your progress. I also recommend keeping a journal. Writing in a journal will allow you to record thoughts, impressions, questions, and ideas in addition to the day-by-day or week-by-week records on the chart. Journals tend to be reflective by nature, and thus they have great value in a process that depends on self-analysis.

Ten Tips for a Habit of Health

In the section above, I presented a six-step process for taking action on a specific issue or stressor. The following tips will help you make good health a lifelong habit.

1. Write out your life goals and how to reach them.

Previously I suggested using a chart or keeping a journal to keep track of your progress toward your goals. Those are good starting points toward implementing this tip. However you do it, the important thing is to set down in some concrete form — write it, draw it, diagram it — what you want out of life and how you plan to achieve it.

I have stressed reflecting on one's goals. Writing makes those reflections less ephemeral and will help when you develop a specific plan of action to achieve those goals. A written plan is easier to stick to and less likely to be ruled by changing emotions. Use your written goals as a road map and stay on course.

2. Look beyond the stress.

Many of us worry before we have reason to. We *anticipate* stress, and we talk ourselves into being stressed.

Often stress comes from fear, either of the unknown or of something we project or anticipate. The dictionary defines *fear* as feeling a threat, real or perceived. One strategy for dealing with anticipatory stress, therefore, is to look beyond the stress, beyond the threat. Treat the anticipated stress as you would view a garden project —look beyond to the flowers. After all, it isn't just about digging, planting, and weeding. It's the flowers we're after. In confronting stress, it is not the battle that matters, it is the victory. In other words, focus on anticipating success in overcoming the stress, not the stressful event itself.

3. Spend time making friends.

Stressors often take hold of us when we feel that we are alone. Having a friend or a group of friends with whom to share your reflections, questions, and plans can make a real difference. Be willing to share the load. Friends can help you come up with proactive ways to reduce stress and to reach wellness goals. And, in turn, you can be the friend who helps another.

4. Practice gratitude for life.

What we want is different from what we need. And, more often than not, it is the wants that lead to feeling stressed. A reflective self-analysis should distinguish the needs and wants. If our needs are largely fulfilled, and most people's are, then developing a sense of gratitude can help mitigate stressful feelings based on un-fulfilled wants. I call this the 98/2 Theory: For most of us, 98% of life is great and 2% is not. Unfortunately, too often we focus on that 2% and ignore the 98%. This tip is about focusing on the 98%.

5. Develop healthy rituals.

Rituals, habits, things we do every day, sometimes without even thinking — these also are worth examining. Consider whether the routine things you do are healthy (stress reducing) or unhealthy (stress inducing). And then work to eliminate the unhealthy ones. For example, in the morning do you grab a cup of coffee or rush through breakfast and then race to work? If so, you're setting yourself up for stress. Why not substitute a healthier ritual, perhaps get up a little earlier, fix a balanced and nutritious breakfast, and give yourself time to linger over the newspaper?

6. Give up show biz.

People who are stressed tend to think they are mind readers. They are always inferring what others mean or projecting: "He thinks I'm. . . ." This tip is about giving up the mind-reader act. Instead, deal with others in a more direct manner. Assumptions lead to misunderstandings and raise the potential for stressful feelings. Don't assume that you know what someone else is thinking or what someone means when they are not clear. Be direct. Ask questions. Engage in meaningful conversation. And, from the opposite side of the exchange, make sure the other person knows what you mean, too.

7. Ask for help.

The old joke is that men never stop to ask for directions, no matter how lost we get. Men and women both fall into that behavior pattern when it comes to asking for directions in life. This tip is a simple one but hard for many people to adopt: Do not be afraid to ask for help. As a kind of life coach, I find more and more professionals coming to me for help in plotting their life paths and exploring what they need to do to reach their goals. Whether the person you turn to is a professional or a caring friend, the point is that sometimes we need help to find balance and direction in life. We should not be reluctant to seek out another human opinion.

Note: In some school districts there are policies regarding stress reduction and access to professional counseling. Find out if your school district has such provisions and use them when you need to.

8. Practice, practice.

Overcoming stress, gaining balance, finding direction, taking action — all of these are skills at which we become better with practice. The more we practice healthy behaviors, the more they become habitual. That is how we adopt habits of health. Sometimes the best way is to find others who are interested in adopting the same good habits. Join a support group or an interest group; attend workshops or participate in teleconferences; hire a personal trainer or a life coach. Explore mentoring. Find a mentor for yourself; become a mentor for someone else. Become a friend.

9. Develop cognitive bumps.

We all experience stress; we all get worked up; we all get depressed. This tip is about moving on, making those periods of stress, anxiety, and depression as short as possible. When we start racing down the road to stress, we need a speed bump to slow us down. A *cognitive bump* is an action you can take to change your focus, to slow you down when you are on the road to being stressed. Some examples of cognitive bumps include: counting to 10, focusing on your breathing (deep and slow), taking a quiet walk, calling a friend, writing a letter, recording your thoughts in a journal.

10. Attend to the physical.

Mental and physical states are linked. We need to attend to both. In the next section I outline what I call "Four Pillars of Health": exercise, diet, rest, and relaxation.

Four Pillars of Health

Physical well-being is important to mental and emotional well-being. Things that stress us can do so more easily if we are tired or poorly nourished. Following are four "pillars" of physical health: exercise, diet, rest, and relaxation. Think of them as supporting the physical edifice of your being.

Exercise. Everyone needs to exercise, especially if physical exercise is not a significant part of daily worklife or if you are faced with stress-producing situations. The exercise itself is less important; it can be walking, cycling, jogging, swimming, or something else. I recommend a combination of aerobic activity and weight training, whether at home or in a gym. Solo workouts are all right, but attending a class, playing on a team, or working out with a partner can bring added benefits.

Diet. Healthy diet recommendations abound, and each person must find the balance that is personally best. My own recommendation is a diet that consists of 35% carbohydrates, 35% proteins, and 30% fat — but it is not what everyone needs. Diets will vary by whether you want to lose weight, gain weight, or simply maintain your weight. On the other hand, most experts agree that most of us drink too little water each day and that we should drink more (eight glasses or more). Often thirst masquerades as hunger, which leads to eating empty calories when we'd be better off downing a glass of water.

Rest. It is important to good mental health (and general alertness) to get enough sleep. For most adults, "enough" is from six to eight hours each night. Most experts agree that striving to maintain consistent retiring and rising times is worthwhile as a way to prevent or cure sleep problems. People are more likely to feel stressed when they are tired.

Relaxation. What a foreign concept relaxation is to most of us. We know about sleep (even when we get too little), but we do not know about relaxation. A powerful stress reducer, relaxation may be as simple as taking a mental walk, meditating, using guided imagery, or any of a dozen other relaxation techniques. Relaxation is a way of stepping back, often from a stressful situation. Many of the cognitive bumps I mentioned in the last section have to do with relaxation.

Conclusion

One of my goals for stress reduction is to work out at the gym each morning before work. I set my task and determine to assess my progress after a month. For 28 days I faithfully get up, throw on sweats, and hit the gym for 40 minutes, combining several aerobic components with weight training. On day 29, however, a problem arises at school and I have to skip my workout to go in early. The problem throws me off my stride, and another day goes by before I can get back to my workout routine. Have I been successful?

What do I focus on: the days I worked out or the days I missed? If I reflect thoughtfully, I know that I must focus on the days I worked out. As a teacher, I can even calculate the percentage: 93%. That's an A in my book.

My point is that everyone experiences setbacks and momentary failures. But I cannot let a 7% failure rate overwhelm a 93% success rate. Even if the success rate is much lower, it will pay to focus on success and build from there. Next time the success will be higher.

In Book II of *The Republic*, Plato comments, "Remember the beginning is the most important part of the work." In this fastback my goal has been to provide ways to begin to address stress and to create wellness. Being a teacher today means that you must learn to deal productively with stress if you are to perform well in the classroom, enjoying not only the experience of teaching but also of living. Teachers who reduce personal stress are better able to present the curriculum and to meet the learning needs of their students. They also model for students the productive, lifelong striving for balance, knowledge, and direction that will serve them in creating wellness for themselves.

References

Brewer, K.C. *The Stress Handbook*. Shawnee Mission, Kans.: National Press Publications, 1991.

Clement, M. "Reducing the Stress of Student Teaching." *Contemporary Education* 70 (Summer 1999): 20.

Covey, S. *The Seven Habits of Highly Successful People*. New York: Simon and Schuster, 1989.

Glasser, W. *Choice Theory: A New Psychology of Personal Freedom*. New York: HarperCollins, 1998.

Glasser, W. *Reality Therapy in Action*. New York: Harper-Collins, 2000.

Hicks, F.R. "The Mental Health of Teachers." Paper presented at George Peabody College for Teachers, Nashville, 1933.

Huling-Austin, L. "Factors to Consider in Alternative Certification Programs: What Can Be Learned from Teacher Induction Research?" *Actions in Teacher Education* 8, no. 2 (1986): 51-58.

Maslach, C. "Burnout: The Cost of Caring." *Journal of Social Issues* 34 (1982): 111-24.

Meichenbaum, D. *Stress Inoculation Training*. Boston: Allyn and Bacon, 1985.

Mosby's Medical, Nursing, & Allied Health Dictionary. 5th ed. New York: Mosby's, 1998.

Nathan, P.E. "Who Should Do Faculty Development and What Should It Be?" *Journal of Counseling and Development* 72, no. 5 (1994): 508.

Peck, L. "A Study of the Adjustment Difficulties of a Group of Women Teachers." *Journal of Educational Psychology* 27 (1936): 401-16.

Schlechty, P., and Vance, V. "Recruitment, Selection, and Retention: The Shape of the Teaching Force." *Elementary School Journal* 83 (1983): 469-87.

Selye, H. *Stress Without Distress*. Philadelphia: J.B. Lippincott, 1974.

Skinner, B.F. *About Behaviorism*. New York: Random House, 1976.

Tracey, B. *The 100 Absolutely Unbreakable Laws of Business Success*. San Francisco: Barrett-Koehler, 2000.

Watkins, C.E. "Burnout in Counseling Practice: Some Potential Professional and Personal Hazards of Becoming a Counselor." *Personal and Guidance Journal* 61 (1983): 304-308.

Recent Books Published by the
Phi Delta Kappa Educational Foundation

100 Classic Books About Higher Education
C. Fincher, G. Keller, E.G. Bogue, and J. Thelin
Trade paperback. $29 (PDK members, $21.75)

Whose Values? Reflections of a New England Prep School Teacher
Barbara Bernache-Baker
Cloth. $49 (PDK members, $38)
Trade paperback. $24 (PDK members, $18)

American Education in the 21st Century
Dan H. Wishnietsky
Trade paperback. $22 (PDK members, $16.50)

Readings on Leadership in Education
From the Archives of Phi Delta Kappa International
Trade paperback. $22 (PDK members, $16.50)

Profiles of Leadership in Education
Mark F. Goldberg
Trade paperback. $22 (PDK members, $16.50)

Use Order Form on Next Page
Or Phone 1-800-766-1156

A processing charge is added to all orders.
Prices are subject to change without notice.

Complete online catalog at http://www.pdkintl.org

Order Form

<table>
<tr><td colspan="3">SHIP TO:</td></tr>
<tr><td colspan="3">STREET</td></tr>
<tr><td colspan="3">CITY/STATE OR PROVINCE/ZIP OR POSTAL CODE</td></tr>
<tr><td colspan="2">DAYTIME PHONE NUMBER</td><td>PDK MEMBER ROLL NUMBER</td></tr>
</table>

QUANTITY	TITLE	PRICE

ORDERS MUST INCLUDE PROCESSING CHARGE

Total Merchandise	Processing Charge
Up to $50	$5
$50.01 to $100	$10
More than $100	$10 plus 5% of total

Special shipping available upon request.
Prices subject to change without notice.

SUBTOTAL	
Indiana residents add 5% Sales Tax	
PROCESSING CHARGE	
TOTAL	

☐ Payment Enclosed (check payable to Phi Delta Kappa International)

Bill my   ☐ VISA   ☐ MasterCard   ☐ American Express   ☐ Discover

| | | | | | | | | | | | | | | | | | | |

ACCT #   DATE

| | | / | | | | |

EXP DATE   SIGNATURE

Mail or fax your order to: Phi Delta Kappa International,
P.O. Box 789, Bloomington, IN 47402-0789. USA
Fax: (812) 339-0018. Phone: (812) 339-1156

**For fastest service, phone 1-800-766-1156
and use your credit card.**